National Preparedness Guidelines

September 2007

PREFACE

President Bush has led a committed effort to strengthen the Nation's preparedness capabilities. The national preparedness architecture encompasses the full spectrum of prevention, protection, response, and recovery efforts to prepare the Nation for all hazards – whether terrorist attack or natural disaster.

Homeland Security Presidential Directive-8 (HSPD-8) of December 17, 2003 (*"National Preparedness"*) directed the Secretary of Homeland Security to develop a national domestic all-hazards preparedness goal. As part of that effort, in March 2005 the Department of Homeland Security (DHS) released the Interim National Preparedness Goal. Publication of the *National Preparedness Guidelines* (*Guidelines*) finalizes development of the national goal and its related preparedness tools.

The *Guidelines*, including the supporting *Target Capabilities List*, simultaneously published online, supersedes the Interim National Preparedness Goal and defines what it means for the Nation to be prepared for all hazards. There are four critical elements of the *Guidelines*:

(1) The **National Preparedness Vision,** which provides a concise statement of the core preparedness goal for the Nation.

(2) The **National Planning Scenarios,** which depict a diverse set of high-consequence threat scenarios of both potential terrorist attacks and natural disasters. Collectively, the 15 scenarios are designed to focus contingency planning for homeland security preparedness work at all levels of government and with the private sector. The scenarios form the basis for coordinated Federal planning, training, exercises, and grant investments needed to prepare for emergencies of all types.

(3) The **Universal Task List (UTL),** which is a menu of some 1,600 unique tasks that can facilitate efforts to prevent, protect against, respond to, and recover from the major events that are represented by the National Planning Scenarios. It presents a common vocabulary and identifies key tasks that support development of essential capabilities among organizations at all levels. Of course, no entity will perform every task.

(4) The **Target Capabilities List (TCL),** which defines 37 specific capabilities that communities, the private sector, and all levels of government should collectively possess in order to respond effectively to disasters.

The *Guidelines* reinforce the fact that preparedness is a shared responsibility. They were developed through an extensive process that involved more than 1,500 Federal, State, and local officials and more than 120 national associations. They also integrate lessons learned following Hurricane Katrina and a 2006 review of States' and major cities' emergency operations and evacuation plans.

Protecting America requires constant vigilance and innovation. These *Guidelines* will shape and support preparedness activities in the months and years ahead, while growing and evolving with the Nation as it strengthens preparedness at all levels of government and within the private sector.

-- *Michael Chertoff*
   Secretary of Homeland Security
   September 2007

TABLE OF CONTENTS

Questions, comments, and suggested improvements related to this document are encouraged. Inquiries, information, and requests for additional copies should be submitted to:

U.S. Department of Homeland Security
Nebraska Avenue Complex
Washington, DC 20528

The National Preparedness Guidelines are available on the
Office for Domestic Preparedness (ODP) Secure Portal (https://odp.esportals.com)
and the Lessons Learned Information Sharing system (https://www.llis.dhs.gov).

For more information on HSPD-8 implementation, go to
http://www.ojp.usdoj.gov/odp/assessments/hspd8.htm

1.0   INTRODUCTION

On December 17, 2003, the President issued HSPD-8. HSPD-8 established national policies to strengthen the preparedness of the United States to prevent, protect against, respond to, and recover from threatened or actual terrorist attacks, major disasters, and other emergencies within the United States. HSPD-8 directed the Secretary of Homeland Security to develop a national domestic all-hazards preparedness goal in coordination with the heads of other appropriate Federal departments and agencies and in consultation with State, local, tribal, and territorial governments. The *National Preparedness Guidelines* (*Guidelines*) finalize development of the national preparedness goal and its related preparedness tools.

The purposes of the *Guidelines* are to:

- Organize and synchronize national (including Federal, State, local, tribal, and territorial) efforts to strengthen national preparedness;

- Guide national investments in national preparedness;

- Incorporate lessons learned from past disasters into national preparedness priorities;

- Facilitate a capability-based and risk-based investment planning process; and

- Establish readiness metrics to measure progress and a system for assessing the Nation's overall preparedness capability to respond to major events, especially those involving acts of terrorism.

The *Guidelines* include a vision, capabilities, and priorities for national preparedness. In order to support a consistent nationwide approach to implementation, the *Guidelines* establish three capabilities-based preparedness tools and a National Preparedness System – all of which are discussed in the sections that follow.

2.0   VISION

The vision for the *National Preparedness Guidelines* is:

> **A NATION PREPARED with coordinated capabilities to prevent, protect against, respond to, and recover from all hazards in a way that balances risk with resources and need.**

This vision is far-reaching. It recognizes that preparedness requires a coordinated national effort involving every level of government, as well as the private sector, nongovernmental organizations, and individual citizens. It addresses capabilities-based preparedness for the full range of homeland security missions, from prevention through recovery. States, communities, and the Federal Government have worked together for decades to manage natural disasters and technological emergencies, particularly with regard to response and recovery. However, they have far less experience with terrorist attacks, particularly with regard to prevention and protection. The *Guidelines* address all hazards and place heavy emphasis on events at the catastrophic end of the risk continuum, especially terrorist attacks, which would require rapid and coordinated national action. The vision acknowledges that the Nation cannot achieve total preparedness for every possible contingency and that no two jurisdictions possess identical capability needs. We must weigh the relative risk of catastrophic events when determining the resources available to address each contingency and the unique needs of each community, determine how to best address needs in light of the risks, and thereby achieve optimal and reasonable levels of preparedness.

2.1 The *Guidelines* Are the Umbrella for a Range of Readiness Initiatives

HSPD-8 is one of several presidential directives that address how the Nation should prepare to prevent, protect against, respond to, and recover from major incidents. Other presidential directives address the evolving threats posed by terrorist attacks and natural disasters.

The *Guidelines* are umbrella documents that collate many plans, strategies, and systems into an overarching framework, the National Preparedness System. Plans and systems will be implemented and requirements will be matched with resources, consistent with applicable law and subject to the availability of appropriations.

Figure 1: The *Guidelines* in Context

2.2   The *Guidelines* Are All-Hazards

As directed by the President in HSPD-8, the *Guidelines* adopt an all-hazards approach to preparedness. An all-hazards approach addresses capabilities-based preparedness to prevent, protect against, respond to, and recover from terrorist attacks, major disasters, and other emergencies.

2.3   The *Guidelines* Are Risk-Based

The *Guidelines* establish a risk-based approach to preparedness. Risk is a function of three variables: threat, vulnerability, and consequence. Both threat and vulnerability are influenced by the probabilities of events that are highly uncertain. In order to compensate for that uncertainty, the *Guidelines* provide a set of National Planning Scenarios that represent a range of threats that warrant national attention. The National Planning Scenarios establish common assumptions to guide planning nationwide regarding potential vulnerabilities and consequences (or impacts) of major incidents. Analysis of the range of potential impacts is essential for defining capabilities in terms of both capacity (i.e., how many are needed) and proficiency (i.e., how well must they be able to perform). These capabilities must be reflected in emergency operations plans (for the near-term) and in preparedness strategies (for the long-term). Federal, State, local, tribal, and territorial officials supplement this approach with risk assessments that provide additional data on their specific threats, vulnerabilities, and consequences. As a result, officials can tailor their approach according to differences in risk across the Nation.

2.4   The *Guidelines* Are a Call to Action

Preparedness is the foundation of successful National Incident Management System (NIMS) implementation. The NIMS places responsibility on individual Federal, State, local, tribal, and territorial governments and agencies for establishing a preparedness cycle in advance of an incident and for including the private sector, non-governmental organizations, and individual citizens, as appropriate. The cycle of preparedness for prevention, protection, response, and recovery missions may be summarized as follows:

- Plan
- Organize and Staff
- Equip
- Train
- Exercise, Evaluate, and Improve

Preparedness is the responsibility of every level of government, every department, and every agency consistent with its authorities. This includes coordinating preparedness activities among partners operating within their jurisdictional borders, as well as across jurisdictional and geographic borders when dictated by identified threats and risk assessments. Preparedness should be coordinated across the same multi-agency coordination entities as described in the NIMS. This is the basis for implementing the *Guidelines*, particularly the national priority to Expand Regional Collaboration (see Section 4.1).

Federal, State, local, tribal, and territorial governments, in cooperation with the private and non-profit sectors, each have a unique role in supporting the preparedness framework established by the *Guidelines*. All levels of government should integrate into their preparedness and response plans the capacity of community, faith-based, and other nongovernmental organizations. This integration includes engaging such organizations in the planning process, providing necessary training and credentialing of their personnel, providing necessary resource support for involvement in a joint response, and incorporating the organizations in training and exercises. Of highest importance is the development of mechanisms for coordination of the volunteers, goods, and services available through these organizations.

The *Guidelines* provide a national framework for a capabilities-based preparedness system and are designed to be measurable so that progress can be determined and specific improvements can be made. Specific metrics and standards are under development for jurisdictions to use when conducting preparedness assessments. Additionally, a process is being established to measure the Nation's overall preparedness. (Guidance on institutionalizing the *Guidelines* is provided within the Secretary's Letter of Instruction in Appendix A.)

3.0   CAPABILITIES

The *Guidelines* establish a capabilities-based approach to preparedness. Simply put, a capability provides the means to accomplish a mission. The *Guidelines* address preparedness for all homeland security mission areas: prevention, protection, response, and recovery. Capabilities are presented alphabetically below by mission area for ease of reference (see Figure 2). Some capabilities cut across all mission areas and are therefore placed in a Common Mission Area.

Figure 2: Capabilities

Common Mission Area	Respond Mission Area
Communications	Animal Health Emergency Support
Community Preparedness and Participation	Citizen Evacuation and Shelter-in-Place
Planning	Critical Resource Logistics and Distribution
Risk Management	Emergency Operations Center Management
Intelligence/Information Sharing and Dissemination	Emergency Public Information and Warning
Prevent Mission Area	Environmental Health
CBRNE Detection	Explosive Device Response Operations
Information Gathering and Recognition of Indicators and Warnings	Fatality Management
Intelligence Analysis and Production	Fire Incident Response Support
Counter-Terror Investigations and Law Enforcement	Isolation and Quarantine

Protect Mission Area	Respond Mission Area *(continued)*
Critical Infrastructure Protection	Mass Care (Sheltering, Feeding, and Related Services)
Epidemiological Surveillance and Investigation	Mass Prophylaxis
Food and Agriculture Safety and Defense	Medical Supplies Management and Distribution
Laboratory Testing	Medical Surge
	Onsite Incident Management
	Emergency Public Safety and Security Response
	Responder Safety and Health
	Emergency Triage and Pre-Hospital Treatment
	Search and Rescue (Land-Based)
	Volunteer Management and Donations
	WMD/Hazardous Materials Response and Decontamination
	Recover Mission Area
	Economic and Community Recovery
	Restoration of Lifelines
	Structural Damage Assessment

Source: Target Capabilities List, as of September 2007

A capability consists of the combination of elements required to deliver the desired outcome. Capability elements are consistent with the NIMS (see Figure 3).

Figure 3: Elements of Capability

Planning	Collection and analysis of intelligence and information, and development of policies, plans, procedures, mutual aid agreements, strategies, and other publications that comply with relevant laws, regulations, and guidance necessary to perform assigned missions and tasks.
Organization and Leadership	Individual teams, an overall organizational structure, and leadership at each level in the structure that comply with relevant laws, regulations, and guidance necessary to perform assigned missions and tasks.
Personnel	Paid and volunteer staff who meet relevant qualification and certification standards necessary to perform assigned missions and tasks.
Equipment and Systems	Major items of equipment, supplies, facilities, and systems that comply with relevant standards necessary to perform assigned missions and tasks.
Training	Content and methods of delivery that comply with relevant training standards necessary to perform assigned missions and tasks.
Exercises, Evaluations, and Corrective Actions	Exercises, self-assessments, peer-assessments, outside reviews, compliance monitoring, and actual major events that provide opportunities to demonstrate, evaluate, and improve the combined capability and interoperability of the other elements to perform assigned missions and tasks to standards necessary to achieve successful outcomes.

Any combination of elements that delivers the desired outcome is acceptable (see Figure 4).

Figure 4: Capabilities and Outcomes
(Listed in Alphabetical Order)

Common

- **Communications**
  Outcome: A continuous flow of critical information is maintained as needed among multi-jurisdictional and multi-disciplinary emergency responders, command posts, agencies, and governmental officials for the duration of the emergency response operation in compliance with the NIMS. In order to accomplish that, the jurisdiction has a continuity of operations plan for public safety communications including the consideration of critical components, networks, support systems, personnel, and an appropriate level of redundant communications systems in the event of an emergency.

- **Community Preparedness and Participation**
  Outcome: There is a structure and a process for ongoing collaboration between government and nongovernmental organizations at all levels; volunteers and nongovernmental resources are incorporated in plans and exercises; the public is educated, trained, and aware; citizens participate in volunteer programs and provide surge capacity support; nongovernmental resources are managed effectively in disasters; and there is a process to evaluate progress.

- **Planning**
  Outcome: Plans incorporate an accurate threat analysis and risk assessment and ensure that capabilities required to prevent, protect against, respond to, and recover from all-hazards events are available when and where they are needed. Plans are vertically and horizontally integrated with appropriate departments, agencies, and jurisdictions. Where appropriate, emergency plans incorporate a mechanism for requesting State and Federal assistance and include a clearly delineated process for seeking and requesting assistance from appropriate agency(ies).

- **Risk Management**
  Outcome: Federal, State, local, tribal, territorial, and private-sector entities identify and assess risks, prioritize and select appropriate protection, prevention, and mitigation solutions based on reduction of risk, monitor the outcomes of allocation decisions, and undertake corrective actions. Additionally, Risk Management is integrated as a planning construct for effective prioritization and oversight of all homeland security investments.

- **Intelligence/Information Sharing and Dissemination**
  Outcome: Effective and timely sharing of information and intelligence occurs across Federal, State, local, tribal, territorial, regional, and private sector entities to achieve coordinated awareness of, prevention of, protection against, and response to a threatened or actual domestic terrorist attack, major disaster, or other emergency.

Prevent Mission Area

- **CBRNE Detection**
  Outcome: Chemical, biological, radiological, nuclear, and/or explosive (CBRNE) materials are rapidly detected and characterized at borders and ports of entry, critical locations, events, and incidents.

- **Information Gathering and Recognition of Indicators and Warnings**
  Outcome: Locally generated threat and other criminal and/or terrorism-related information is identified, gathered, entered into an appropriate data/retrieval system, and provided to appropriate analysis centers.

- **Intelligence Analysis and Production**
  Outcome: Timely, accurate, and actionable intelligence/information products are produced in support of prevention, awareness, deterrence, response, and continuity planning operations.

- **Counter-Terror Investigations and Law Enforcement**
  Outcome: Suspects involved in criminal activities related to homeland security are successfully deterred, detected, disrupted, investigated, and apprehended. All counterterrorism-related cases are aggressively prosecuted.

Protect Mission Area

- **Critical Infrastructure Protection**
  Outcome: The risk to, vulnerability of, and consequence of an attack on critical infrastructure are reduced through the identification of critical infrastructure; conduct, documentation, and standardization of risk assessments; prioritization of assets; decisions regarding protective and preventative programs; and implementation of protective and preventative plans.

- **Epidemiological Surveillance and Investigation**
  Outcome: Potential exposure to disease is identified rapidly by determining exposure and mode of transmission and agent; interrupting transmission to contain the spread of the event; and reducing number of cases. Confirmed cases are reported immediately to all relevant public health, food regulatory, environmental regulatory, and law enforcement agencies. Suspected cases are investigated promptly, reported to relevant public health authorities, and accurately confirmed to ensure appropriate preventive or curative countermeasures are implemented. An outbreak is defined and characterized; new suspect cases are identified and characterized based on case definitions on an ongoing basis; relevant clinical specimens are obtained and transported for confirmatory laboratory testing; the source of exposure is tracked; methods of transmission identified; and effective mitigation measures are communicated to the public, providers, and relevant agencies, as appropriate.

- **Food and Agriculture Safety and Defense**
  Outcome: Threats to food and agricultural safety are prevented, mitigated, and eradicated; affected products are disposed of; affected facilities are decontaminated; public and plant health are protected; notification of the event and instructions of appropriate actions are effectively communicated with all stakeholders; trade in agricultural products is restored safely; and confidence in the U.S. food supply is maintained.

- **Public Health Laboratory Testing**
  Outcome: Chemical, radiological, and biological agents causing, or having the potential to cause, widespread illness or death are rapidly detected and accurately identified by the public health laboratory within the jurisdiction or through network collaboration with other appropriate Federal, State, and local laboratories. The public health laboratory, working in close partnership with public health epidemiology, environmental health, law enforcement, agriculture and veterinary officials, hospitals, and other appropriate agencies, produces timely and accurate data to support ongoing public health investigations and the implementation of appropriate preventative or curative countermeasures.

Respond Mission Area

- **Animal Disease Emergency Support**
  Outcome: Foreign animal disease is prevented from entering the United States by protecting the related critical infrastructure and key assets. In the event of an incident, animal disease is detected

as early as possible, exposure of livestock to foreign diseases is reduced, immediate and humane actions to eradicate the outbreak are implemented, public and animal health and the environment are protected, continuity of agriculture and related business is safely maintained and/or restored, and economic damage is minimized. Trade in agricultural products and domestic and international confidence in the U.S. food supply are safely maintained or restored.

- **Citizen Evacuation and Shelter-In-Place**
Outcome: Affected and at-risk populations (and companion animals to the extent necessary to save human lives) are safely sheltered-in-place or evacuated to safe refuge areas.

- **Critical Resource Logistics and Distribution**
Outcome: Critical resources are available to incident managers and emergency responders upon request for proper distribution and to aid disaster victims in a cost-effective and timely manner.

- **Emergency Operations Center Management**
Outcome: The event is effectively managed through multi-agency coordination for a pre-planned or no-notice event.

- **Emergency Public Information and Warning**
Outcome: Government agencies and public and private sector entities receive and transmit coordinated, prompt, useful, and reliable information regarding threats to their health, safety, and property, through clear, consistent information-delivery systems. This information is updated regularly and outlines protective measures that can be taken by individuals and their communities.

- **Environmental Health**
Outcome: After the primary event, disease and injury are prevented through the quick identification of associated environmental hazards, including exposure to infectious diseases that are secondary to the primary event as well as secondary transmission modes. The at-risk population (i.e., exposed or potentially exposed) receives the appropriate countermeasures, including treatment or protection, in a timely manner. The rebuilding of the public health infrastructure, removal of environmental hazards, and appropriate decontamination of the environment enable the safe re-entry and re-occupancy of the impacted area. Continued monitoring occurs throughout the recovery process in order to identify hazards and reduce exposure.

- **Explosive Device Response Operations**
Outcome: Threat assessments are conducted, the explosive and/or hazardous devices are rendered safe, and the area is cleared of hazards. Measures are implemented in the following priority order: ensure public safety; safeguard the officers on the scene (including the bomb technician); collect and preserve evidence; protect and preserve public and private property; and restore public services.

- **Fatality Management**
Outcome: Complete documentation and recovery of human remains and items of evidence (except in cases where the health risks posed to personnel outweigh the benefits of recovery of remains). Remains receive surface decontamination (if indicated) and, unless catastrophic circumstances dictate otherwise, are examined, identified, and released to the next-of-kin's funeral home with a complete certified death certificate. Reports of missing persons and ante mortem data are efficiently collected. Victims' family members receive updated information prior to the media release. All hazardous material regulations are reviewed and any restrictions on the transportation and disposition of remains are made clear by those with the authority and responsibility to establish the standards. Law enforcement agencies are given all information needed to investigate and prosecute the case successfully. Families are provided incident-specific support services.

- **Fire Incident Response Support**
Outcome: Dispatch and safe arrival of the initial fire suppression resources occur within jurisdictional

response time objectives. The first unit to arrive initiates the Incident Command System (ICS), assesses the incident scene, communicates the situation, and requests appropriate resources including any necessary mutual aid or cross-discipline support. Firefighting activities are conducted safely and fire hazards are contained, controlled, extinguished, and investigated, and the incident is managed in accordance with emergency response plans and procedures.

- **Isolation and Quarantine**
  Outcome: Individuals who are ill, exposed, or likely to be exposed are separated, movement is restricted, basic necessities of life are available, and their health is monitored in order to limit the spread of a newly introduced contagious disease (e.g., pandemic influenza). Legal authority for those measures is clearly defined and communicated to all responding agencies and the public. Logistical support is provided to maintain measures until danger of contagion has elapsed.

- **Mass Care (Sheltering, Feeding, and Related Services)**
  Outcome: Mass care services, including sheltering, feeding, and bulk distribution, are rapidly provided for the population and companion animals within the affected area.

- **Mass Prophylaxis**
  Outcome: Appropriate drug prophylaxis and vaccination strategies are implemented in a timely manner upon the onset of an event to prevent the development of disease in exposed individuals. Public information strategies include recommendations on specific actions individuals can take to protect their family, friends, and themselves.

- **Medical Supplies Management and Distribution**
  Outcome: Critical medical supplies and equipment are appropriately secured, managed, distributed, and restocked in a timeframe appropriate to the incident.

- **Medical Surge**
  Outcome: Injured or ill from the event are rapidly and appropriately cared for. Continuity of care is maintained for non-incident related illness or injury.

- **Onsite Incident Management**
  Outcome: The event is managed safely, effectively, and efficiently through the common framework of the ICS.

- **Emergency Public Safety and Security Response**
  Outcome: The incident scene is assessed and secured; access is controlled; security support is provided to other response operations (and related critical locations, facilities, and resources); emergency public information is provided while protecting first responders and mitigating any further public risks; and any crime/incident scene preservation issues are addressed.

- **Responder Safety and Health**
  Outcome: No illnesses or injury to any first responder, first receiver, medical facility staff member, or other skilled support personnel as a result of preventable exposure to secondary trauma, chemical/radiological release, infectious disease, or physical and emotional stress after the initial incident or during decontamination and incident follow-up.

- **Emergency Triage and Pre-Hospital Treatment**
  Outcome: Emergency Medical Services (EMS) resources are effectively and appropriately dispatched and provide pre-hospital triage, treatment, transport, tracking of patients, and documentation of care appropriate for the incident, while maintaining the capabilities of the EMS system for continued operations.

- **Search and Rescue (Land-Based)**
  Outcome: The greatest numbers of victims (human and, to the extent that no humans remain endangered, animal) are rescued and transferred to medical or mass care capabilities, in the shortest amount of time, while maintaining rescuer safety.

- **Volunteer Management and Donations**
  Outcome: The positive effect of using unaffiliated volunteers and unsolicited donations is maximized and does not hinder response and recovery activities.

- **WMD/Hazardous Materials Response and Decontamination**
  Outcome: Any hazardous materials release is rapidly identified and mitigated; victims exposed to the hazard are rescued, decontaminated, and treated; the impact of the release is limited; and responders and at-risk populations are effectively protected.

Recover Mission Area

- **Economic and Community Recovery**
  Outcome: Economic impact is estimated; priorities are set for recovery activities; business disruption is minimized; and individuals and families are provided with appropriate levels and types of relief with minimal delay.

- **Restoration of Lifelines**
  Outcome: Lifelines to undertake sustainable emergency response and recovery activities are established.

- **Structural Damage Assessment**
  Outcome: Accurate situation needs and damage assessments occur. The full range of engineering, building inspection, and enforcement services are implemented, managed, and coordinated in a way that maximizes the use of resources, aids emergency response, and implements recovery operations. Mitigation projects to lessen the impact of similar future events are identified and prioritized.

Source: Target Capabilities List, as of September 2007

The challenge for government officials, working with the private sector, nongovernmental organizations, and individual citizens, is to determine the best way to build capabilities for bolstering preparedness and achieving the *Guidelines*. The "best way" will vary across the Nation. In order to assist officials in that effort, the *Guidelines* establish a Capabilities-Based Preparedness process and three planning tools: the *National Planning Scenarios*; the *Target Capabilities List* (TCL); and the *Universal Task List* (UTL), which are discussed in detail in Appendix B. The *National Planning Scenarios* are designed to identify the broad spectrum of tasks and capabilities needed for all-hazards preparedness. The TCL is a comprehensive catalog of capabilities to perform homeland security missions, including performance measures and metrics for common tasks. The UTL is a library and hierarchy of tasks by homeland security mission area. Capabilities-Based Preparedness encourages flexibility and requires collaboration. More importantly, it helps to ensure that operations planners and program managers across the Nation can use common tools and processes when making planning, training, equipment, and other investments, and can produce measurable results. For more information on how the *Guidelines* contribute to the development of specific homeland security capabilities, please refer to Appendix B.

4.0   PRIORITIES

HSPD-8 directs that the *Guidelines* establish measurable readiness priorities and targets. The *Guidelines* include a series of national priorities to guide preparedness efforts that meet the Nation's most urgent needs (see Figure 5). The priorities reflect major themes and recurring issues identified in national strategies, presidential directives, State and Urban Area Homeland Security Strategies, the Hurricane Katrina Reports, and other lessons-learned reports. The priorities will be updated or refined over time as we implement the *Guidelines* or encounter changes in the homeland security strategic environment.

Figure 5: National Priorities and Associated Capabilities

National Priority	Associated Capabilities
Expand Regional Collaboration	Multiple capabilities
Implement the National Incident Management System and National Response Plan	Multiple capabilities
Implement the National Infrastructure Protection Plan	Multiple capabilities
Strengthen Information Sharing and Collaboration Capabilities	Intelligence/Information Sharing and Dissemination Counter-Terror Investigations and Law Enforcement
Strengthen Interoperable and Operable Communications Capabilities	Communications Emergency Public Information and Warning
Strengthen CBRNE Detection, Response, and Decontamination Capabilities	CBRNE Detection Explosive Device Response Operations WMD/Hazardous Materials Response and Decontamination
Strengthen Medical Surge and Mass Prophylaxis Capabilities	Medical Surge Mass Prophylaxis
Strengthen Planning and Citizen Preparedness Capabilities	Planning Citizen Evacuation and Shelter-in-Place Mass Care (Sheltering, Feeding, and Related Services) Community Preparedness and Participation

Federal departments and agencies are required to review the national priorities periodically in order to ensure that Federal preparedness programs and initiatives support their implementation. They are also required to provide information on specific, concrete actions that will demonstrate progress in achieving these priorities in their annual program guidance. A brief discussion of the national priorities follows, including examples of major Federal programs that support each priority.

4.1 Expand Regional Collaboration

National Priority: Standardized structures and processes for regional collaboration enable entities collectively to manage and coordinate activities for operations and preparedness consistently and effectively.

Discussion: Regional collaboration is critical to improving preparedness and achieving the tenets set forth in the *Guidelines*. As used in this document, a "region" generally refers to a geographic area consisting of contiguous Federal, State, local, tribal, and territorial jurisdictions. Major events often have regional impact; therefore, prevention, protection, response, and recovery missions require extensive regional collaboration. It is vital to enhance efforts by Federal, State, local, tribal, and territorial entities to communicate and coordinate with one another, the private sector, nongovernmental organizations, and individual citizens. The intent is to identify geographic regions that work best for achieving and sustaining coordinated capabilities and mutual aid agreements. Federal departments and agencies should foster those regional groupings through planning and Federal preparedness assistance. Formal arrangements among geographic regions will enable the Federal Government, working with States, territories, local, and tribal governments and other partners, to coordinate preparedness activities more effectively, spread costs, pool resources, disburse risk, and thereby increase the overall return on investment.

One example of an initiative that supports this priority is the Urban Areas Security Initiative (UASI) managed by DHS. This initiative focuses on a limited number of high-threat urban areas. The UASI also includes multi-jurisdictional metropolitan regions identified by States that do not have a designated urban area. Another example is the Cities Readiness Initiative (CRI), led by the Department of Health and Human Services (HHS) through the Centers for Disease Control and Prevention (CDC) in collaboration with the United States Postal Service. This initiative focuses on selected cities to help them prepare to provide life-saving interventions through the timely delivery of medicines and medical supplies during a large-scale public health emergency. The Emergency Management Assistance Compact (EMAC), a State-to-State partnership coordinated by the National Emergency Management Association (NEMA), also supports this priority. The EMAC was congressionally ratified in 1996 to provide a fast and flexible response system through which States send requested personnel and equipment to help disaster relief efforts in other States. All 50 States, the District of Columbia, Puerto Rico, and the U.S. Virgin Islands have enacted legislation to become members of the EMAC. During Hurricane Katrina, EMAC provided interstate mutual aid in the response effort by deploying more than 67,000 personnel to Louisiana and Mississippi.

Additional information on Homeland Security Grant Programs such as UASI can be found online at: http://www.ojp.usdoj.gov/odp/grants_programs.htm

Additional information on the Cities Readiness Initiative can be found online at: http://www.bt.cdc.gov/cri/

Additional information on the EMAC can be found online at: http://www.emacweb.org

4.2   Implement the National Incident Management System and National Response Plan

National Priority: The National Incident Management System (NIMS) and National Response Plan (NRP) are fully implemented nationwide and support the coordinated development of capabilities.

Discussion: Homeland Security Presidential Directive-5 (HSPD-5) (*"Management of Domestic Incidents"*) of February 28, 2003, mandated the development of the NIMS and the NRP. The NIMS, released in March 2004, provides a consistent framework for government entities at all levels to work together to manage domestic incidents, regardless of cause, size, or complexity. The NIMS includes a core set of guidelines, standards, and protocols for command and management, preparedness, resource management, communications and information management, supporting technologies, and coordination and maintenance to promote interoperability and compatibility among Federal, State, local, tribal, and territorial capabilities.

The NRP, using the template established by the NIMS, was released in December 2004. The NRP is an all-discipline, all-hazards plan that establishes a single, comprehensive framework for the management of domestic incidents. It provides the structure and mechanisms for evolving or potential incidents requiring a coordinated Federal response. The NRP is always in effect. However, the NRP coordinating structures and processes are flexible and scalable and can be activated at different levels depending on the nature of the threat or incident. Actions range in scope from ongoing situational reporting and analysis, through the implementation of NRP Incident Annexes and other supplemental Federal contingency plans, to full implementation of all relevant NRP coordination mechanisms.

In May 2006, DHS published a Notice of Change to the NRP in order to address a limited number of issues requiring amendments prior to the official review of the NRP. The alterations, or in some cases, clarifications, were based on lessons learned from exercises and real-world events. The modifications in the Notice of Change strengthened national doctrine and operating concepts for incidents requiring a coordinated Federal response. All Federal departments and agencies, and other NRP signatories, are required to implement and operate under the concepts of the NRP.

Since then, DHS has worked closely with stakeholders to revise the National Response Plan (NRP). Because the issues are complex and require national-level policy decisions, DHS is working on an updated document that addresses the roles and responsibilities of stakeholders and incident management structures. DHS will release the new draft of the NRP once stakeholders have been able to review and comment on the document. In the meantime, the structures and mechanisms of the original NRP, with modifications from the May 2006 Notice of Change, are still intact and should be used for any hazard or threat occurring prior to the approval and release of the revised NRP.

Additional information on the NIMS can be found online at:
http://www.fema.gov/emergency/nims/

Additional information on the NRP can be found online at:
http://www.dhs.gov/dhspublic/interapp/editorial/editorial_0566.xml

4.3   Implement the National Infrastructure Protection Plan

National Priority: The National Infrastructure Protection Plan (NIPP) is fully implemented nationwide and supports the coordinated development of critical infrastructure protection capabilities.

Discussion: The Homeland Security Act of 2002 directs DHS to ensure the protection of the Nation's critical infrastructure and key resources (CI/KR). Homeland Security Presidential Directive-7 (HSPD-7) (*"Critical Infrastructure Identification, Prioritization, and Protection"*) of December 17, 2003, directed the Secretary of Homeland Security to establish a national plan, working closely with other Federal departments and agencies, State, local, tribal, and territorial governments, and the private sector, to unify the Nation's efforts to protect CI/KR. The NIPP is the comprehensive risk management framework that clearly defines critical infrastructure protection roles and responsibilities for all levels of government, private industry, nongovernmental agencies, and tribal partners. The NIPP lays out the plan for setting requirements for infrastructure protection, which will help ensure our government, economy, and public services continue in the event of a terrorist attack or other disaster. The NIPP was released on June 30, 2006. The purpose of the NIPP is to "build a safer, more secure, and more resilient America by enhancing protection of the Nation's CI/KR to prevent, deter, neutralize, or mitigate the effects of deliberate efforts by terrorists to destroy, incapacitate, or exploit them; and to strengthen national preparedness, timely response, and rapid recovery in the event of an attack, natural disaster, or other emergency."

Achieving that national priority requires meeting a series of objectives that include: understanding and sharing information about terrorist threats and other hazards; building security partnerships; implementing a long-term risk management program; and maximizing the efficient use of resources. Measuring progress toward implementing the NIPP requires that CI/KR security partners have the following:

- Coordinated, risk-based CI/KR plans and programs in place addressing known and potential threats;

- Structures and processes that are flexible and adaptable, both to incorporate operational lessons learned and effective practices, and also to adapt quickly to a changing threat or incident environment;

- Processes in place to identify and address dependencies and interdependencies to allow for more timely and effective implementation of short-term protective actions and more rapid response and recovery; and

- Access to robust information-sharing networks that include relevant intelligence, threat analysis, and real-time incident reporting.

The NIPP details actions to accomplish the following:

- Implement a risk management framework to guide CI/KR protection programs and activities;

- Strengthen linkages between physical and cyber, as well as domestic and international CI/KR protection efforts;

- Enhance and sustain information sharing and public-private sector coordination;

- Integrate steady-state CI/KR protection programs in an all-hazards environment;

- Integrate CI/KR protection as part of the homeland security mission;

- Maximize efficient use of resources for CI/KR protection; and

- Achieve an effective and efficient national CI/KR protection program over the longer term.

Sector-Specific Plans (SSPs) detail each sector's specific approach for executing the NIPP risk management framework, including setting sector security supporting goals, inventorying assets, assessing risks, prioritizing assets, implementing protective programs, and measuring progress toward CI/KR protection.

For more information, the NIPP is available online at: www.dhs.gov/nipp

Comments and questions can be sent to: NIPP@dhs.gov

4.4   Strengthen Information Sharing and Collaboration Capabilities

National Priority: Information sharing and collaboration capabilities are developed to target levels in the States, tribal areas, territories, and designated urban areas that are consistent with measures and metrics established in the TCL.

Discussion: This national priority focuses on the Intelligence and Information Sharing and Dissemination and the Counter-Terror Investigations and Law Enforcement capabilities outlined in the TCL. It is also closely linked to the national priority to Strengthen Interoperable and Operable Communications Capabilities (see Section 4.5). A common operating picture can only be achieved through a national information management system supported by an operational interoperable communications network.

The Intelligence and Information Sharing and Dissemination capability refers to the multi-jurisdictional, multidisciplinary exchange and dissemination of information and intelligence among entities at all levels of government, as well as nongovernmental organizations, the private sector, and citizens. Intelligence is derived by gathering, analyzing, and fusing relevant information from a wide range of sources on a continual basis. Successful homeland security efforts require a national information management system that provides an effective and seamless capability to gather, analyze, disseminate, and use information regarding threats, vulnerabilities, and consequences to support prevention and response efforts. As the response to

Hurricane Katrina demonstrated, prompt and effective information sharing and reporting is essential for response activities. Successful responses are dependent upon real-time, accurate situational awareness of both the facts from the disaster area and ongoing response activities. Strengthened information sharing and collaboration capabilities will enable a more accurate situational awareness and allow development of a real-time common operating picture. To support these efforts, government departments and agencies need a single reporting system (or system of systems) to ensure critical information reaches the appropriate decision-makers and the public in a timely manner. The Law Enforcement Investigation and Operations Counter-Terror Investigations and Law Enforcement capability contributes to successful deterrence, detection, disruption, investigation, and apprehension of suspects involved in terrorism and related criminal activities. Law enforcement and other appropriate personnel must be partners in the Intelligence and Information Sharing and Dissemination capability to conduct successful investigations.

The President and the Congress have directed the creation of an Information Sharing Environment (ISE) to provide and facilitate the means for sharing terrorism information among all appropriate Federal, State, local, tribal, and territorial governments, as well as private sector entities, through the issuance of policy guidelines and technologies. A number of Federal initiatives support this national priority, including the following:

- Establishment of an ISE Program Manager position in the Office of the Director of National Intelligence. On November 16, 2006, the Director of National Intelligence delivered the ISE Implementation Plan to the Congress. The report provides a vision, strategy, and roadmap for developing a comprehensive implementation plan and outlines the activities to be undertaken by the ISE Program Manager, Federal departments and agencies, State, local, tribal, and territorial governments, and private sector entities.

- Establishment of the Information Sharing and Collaboration Office within DHS to serve as the DHS focal point for information sharing policy, coordination, and implementation both within DHS and with the Department's partners to achieve effective information sharing and collaboration.

- Embedding intelligence and operational personnel from the DHS Office of Intelligence and Analysis in State and local fusion centers. These deployed professionals will facilitate the flow of timely, actionable, all-hazard information across State and local governments as well as the national intelligence and law enforcement communities.

- Expansion of the Homeland Security Information Network, managed by DHS, to strengthen the real-time, collaborative information flow among homeland security partners.

- Establishment of the Law Enforcement Information Sharing Program, which provides data exchange services that enhance the information-sharing capabilities of the Department of Justice (DOJ). One component of that capability is provided by the Joint Terrorism Task Forces (JTTF), led by the Federal Bureau of Investigation (FBI). The JTTF enhances communication, coordination, and cooperation among agencies at all levels of government representing intelligence, law enforcement, defense, diplomatic, public safety, and homeland security disciplines by providing a point of fusion for terrorism intelligence. Another component of this capability is provided by the Anti-

Terrorism Advisory Councils led by the U.S. Attorneys, which also facilitate information sharing among law enforcement organizations at all levels of government.

Additional information on the Homeland Security Information Network can be found online at: http://www.dhs.gov/xinfoshare/programs/gc_1156888108137.shtm

Additional information on FBI and related DOJ efforts in this area can be found online at: http://www.fbi.gov/terrorinfo/counterrorism/waronterrorhome.htm

Additional information on the ISE can be found online at: http://www.ise.gov

4.5   Strengthen Interoperable and Operable Communications Capabilities

National Priority: Interoperable and operable communications capabilities are developed to target levels in the States, tribal areas, territories, and designated urban areas that are consistent with measures and metrics established in the TCL.

Discussion: This national priority focuses on the communications capability from the TCL. Communications interoperability is the ability of public safety agencies (including police, fire, EMS, etc.) and service agencies (including public works, transportation, hospitals, etc.) to talk within and across agencies and jurisdictions via radio and associated communications systems; exchange voice, data, and/or video with one another on demand; and do so in real time, when needed, and when authorized.

Prior disasters and emergencies, as well as State and Urban Area Homeland Security Strategies and status reports on interoperable communications, have shown persistent shortfalls in achieving communications interoperability. These shortfalls demonstrate a need for a national framework fostering the identification of communications requirements and definition of technical standards. State and local authorities, working in partnership with DHS, need to establish statewide interoperable communications plans and a national interoperability baseline to assess the current state of communications interoperability. Achieving interoperable communications and creating effective mechanisms for sharing information are long-term projects that require Federal leadership and a collaborative approach to planning that involves all levels of government as well as the private sector.

DHS recently established the Office of Emergency Communications (OEC) to integrate and coordinate the Department's interoperable communications programs. OEC now manages the Interoperable Communications Technical Assistance Program (ICTAP), the interoperable communications policy development component of SAFECOM, and the Integrated Wireless Network (IWN) program. ICTAP provides direct technical assistance to State, local, tribal, and territorial emergency responders and public safety officials in coordination with the UASI grant program (see section 4.1 above). ICTAP leverages and works with other Federal, State, local, tribal, and territorial interoperability efforts to enhance the overall capacity for agencies and individuals to communicate. SAFECOM promotes, coordinates, and provides assistance to the efforts of Federal, State, local, tribal, and territorial public safety agencies to strengthen interoperable communications capabilities. SAFECOM emphasizes a practitioner-driven approach in addressing communications interoperability. IWN is a collaborative effort by the Departments of the Treasury, Justice, and Homeland Security, to provide a consolidated nationwide Federal wireless communications system with integrated services (voice, data, and multimedia) in support of first responder and homeland security missions.

The Nationwide Interoperable Communications Baseline Survey and Tactical Interoperable Communications Plan initiatives confirm that successful interoperability lies in the development of governance structures, standard operating procedures, training and exercises, and well-defined usage of interoperable communications.

Additional information on SAFECOM can be found online at:
http://www.safecomprogram.gov/SAFECOM

Additional information on IWN can be found online at: http://www.usdoj.gov/jmd/iwn/

Additional information on TICP can be found online at:
http://www.ojp.usdoj.gov/odp/ta_ictap.htm

Additional information on the Nationwide Interoperable Communications Baseline Survey can be found online at:
http://www.safecomprogram.gov/SAFECOM/library/background/1295_2006national.htm

4.6   Strengthen CBRNE Detection, Response, and Decontamination Capabilities

National Priority: Chemical, biological, radiological, nuclear, and explosive (CBRNE) detection, response, and decontamination capabilities are developed to target levels in the States, tribal areas, territories, and designated urban areas that are consistent with measures and metrics established in the TCL.

Discussion: This national priority focuses on three capabilities from the TCL: CBRNE Detection; Explosive Device Response Operations; and Weapons of Mass Destruction (WMD) and Hazardous Materials Response and Decontamination. The National Security Strategy issued in March 2006 notes that there are few threats greater than a terrorist attack with WMD. CBRNE materials can be used as WMD to produce thousands of casualties in a single attack. The Nation's capability to detect and respond to such incidents is imperative. Because the potential number of terrorist targets is large, and the threats and means of delivery are varied, the Nation must develop a layered defense against WMD. An effective CBRNE detection infrastructure will ensure CBRNE materials are rapidly detected, identified, and safely managed at borders, critical locations, events, and incidents. By their nature, CBRNE materials differ in detection and characterization methodologies. CBRNE response includes activities to address the immediate and short-term actions to preserve life, property, and the environment, as well as the social, economic, and political structure of the community, State, and Nation. It is critical that all levels of government coordinate the development of interagency response protocols prior to the deployment of detection technology. Additional response activities are required post-release/detonation. The ability to rapidly decontaminate large numbers of affected persons is critical in preventing injury or death.

This national priority leverages efforts throughout government to develop capabilities to detect, neutralize, contain, dismantle, and dispose of CBRNE materials, and decontaminate exposed personnel and property. State, local, tribal, and territorial agencies and their hazardous materials response teams are key players in early detection, response, and decontamination. At the Federal level, different departments and agencies are key players for aspects of CBRNE detection, response, and decontamination. These include the following: the Departments of Defense, Justice, Agriculture, Health and Human Services, Energy, and Homeland Security; the Environmental Protection Agency; and the Nuclear Regulatory Commission.

Additional information on the NRP as it relates to CBRNE can be found online at: http://www.dhs.gov/nationalresponseplan

4.7 Strengthen Medical Surge and Mass Prophylaxis Capabilities

National Priority: Medical surge and mass prophylaxis capabilities are developed to target levels in the States, tribal areas, territories, and designated urban areas that are consistent with measures and metrics established in the TCL.

Discussion: This national priority focuses on the Medical Surge and Mass Prophylaxis capabilities outlined in the TCL. The Medical Surge and Mass Prophylaxis capabilities are the first lines of response to bioterrorism, pandemic influenza, and other public health emergencies. The Medical Surge capability is prioritized because of the urgent need to enable our healthcare system, particularly hospitals, to handle large numbers of patients requiring immediate hospitalization following any type of incident. The ability to triage and provide decontamination when necessary is essential. Emergency-ready hospitals and other healthcare entities must be able to work collectively to handle different types of injuries, including physical and psychological trauma, burns, infections, bone marrow suppression, or other chemical- or radiation-induced injuries. Finally, in anticipation of a mass casualty incident that exceeds the aggregate surge capacity of local hospitals, the community of medical providers must have provisions in place to immediately accommodate an influx of supplemental healthcare assets from mutual-aid partners, States, and the Federal Government. The Mass Prophylaxis capability requires public health departments to organize and direct a mass prophylaxis campaign within an extremely short timeframe, should one be needed to prevent illness and/or death in the face of a potential or actual mass casualty incident. A mass prophylaxis campaign would require more staff than what is normally available at a public health department to fulfill all functional roles. Therefore, it is critical to involve other staffing sources (e.g., first responders, nongovernmental organizations, and volunteers) in the campaign. The Cities Readiness Initiative is a pilot project to assist cities in increasing their capacity to deliver medicines and supplies for mass prophylaxis during a large-scale public health emergency (see Section 4.1). HHS provides many Federal programs that support this priority. Two of the 12 HHS readiness objectives for State and local public health emergency preparedness support this priority. The Public Health Security and Bioterrorism Preparedness and Response Act of 2002 addresses the need to enhance public health and healthcare readiness for bioterrorism and other public health emergencies. The Nation needs emergency-ready public health and healthcare services in every community as a first line of response to such threats.

Also, as envisioned in the NRP and "*Biodefense for the 21st Century*," the Nation needs to strengthen Federal capabilities (such as the National Disaster Medical System and the Strategic National Stockpile) to assist and augment State, local, tribal, and territorial emergency response efforts as necessary, especially in responding to mass casualty incidents. Within HHS, the Office of the Secretary administers the National Bioterrorism Hospital Preparedness Program. This program enhances the ability of the Nation's hospitals and the healthcare system to prepare for and respond to bioterrorism and other public health emergencies. The CDC administers the Cooperative Agreement on Public Health Preparedness and Response for Bioterrorism. CDC funds are intended to upgrade State and local public health jurisdictions' preparedness for and response to the priorities identified in authorizing legislation.

Additional information on HHS readiness priorities can be found online at: http://www.hhs.gov/ophep/npgs.html

Additional information on Medical Surge can be found online at: http://www.hrsa.gov/bioterrorism/

Additional information on Mass Prophylaxis can be found on the CDC Coordinating Office of Terrorism Preparedness and Emergency Response website at: http://www.bt.cdc.gov

4.8   Community Preparedness: Strengthening Planning and Citizen Capabilities

National Priority: Planning and citizen preparedness capabilities are developed to target levels in the States, tribal areas, territories, and designated urban areas that are consistent with measures and metrics established in the TCL.

Discussion: This national priority focuses on the Planning, Citizen Evacuation and Shelter-in-Place, Mass Care (sheltering, feeding, and related services), and Community Preparedness and Participation capabilities from the TCL. Hurricane Katrina demonstrated not only the need for renewed emphasis on planning capabilities, especially emergency operations planning, but also on citizen preparedness. In a speech from Jackson Square in New Orleans after Hurricane Katrina, President Bush highlighted emergency planning as a "national security priority." The Nation's homeland security system is highly complex, with multiple objectives, partners, and needs. Plans help make sense of this complex homeland environment. Planning is a methodical way to think through the entire life-cycle of a potential crisis. Good planning repays the investment of time and effort in development and rehearsal by shortening the time required to gain control over an incident and by providing favorable conditions for rapid and effective exchange of information about a situation, its analysis, and alternative responses. Planning helps Federal, State, local, tribal, and territorial governments reorient capabilities and resources to be more agile and ensures organizational structures, processes, and procedures effectively support the intended strategic direction. As stakeholders learn and practice their roles, they can reduce uncertainty, expedite response, and improve effectiveness during the critical initial stages after an event. This effort is a key to success in protecting people and property in crises.

The DHS Appropriations Act of 2006 directed DHS to complete a comprehensive nationwide review of catastrophic planning, including planning for mass evacuations, sheltering, and related services. DHS completed the Nationwide Plan Review in June 2006. The first phase of the effort included analysis and reporting from States, territories, and urban areas regarding the status of their plans, including when their plans were last updated and their confidence in the plans to manage a catastrophic event. The second phase involved a peer review, validation of the self-assessments, determination of requirements for planning assistance, and identification of initial conclusions for strengthening plans for catastrophic events. The Nationwide Plan Review was an initial step in establishing a shared contingency planning process to develop sound plans that describe in detail how Federal, State, and local governments will jointly accomplish their respective missions and employ the full range of capabilities at their disposal to achieve overall national objectives.

As uniformed emergency responders constitute less than one percent of the total U.S. population, it is clear that citizens must be better prepared, trained, and practiced on how best to take care of themselves and assist others in those first, crucial hours during and after a catastrophic incident. Citizens can reduce the demand for emergency assistance during catastrophic incidents through preparedness measures and actively contribute to the Nation's response capability by participating in response and recovery activities. A trained and involved public will provide the Nation with a critical surge capacity to augment government efforts in a catastrophic incident. During Hurricane Katrina, many citizens exercised appropriate precautionary and response actions and many citizens volunteered to support the response and recovery efforts. In February 2006, the White House released "*The Federal Response to Hurricane Katrina: Lessons Learned*," which emphasizes that "citizen and community preparedness are among the most effective means of preventing terrorist attacks, as well as protecting against, mitigating, responding to, and recovering from all hazards. . . .[i]f every family developed their own emergency preparedness plan, they almost certainly would reduce the demand for outside emergency resources." Through the *Ready Campaign* and the nationwide network of State and local Citizen Corps Councils, DHS will focus on strengthening citizen preparedness capabilities, particularly for special needs and socially vulnerable populations.

Additional information on FEMA and Planning can be found online at:
http://www.fema.gov/plan/

Additional information on planning standards can be found online at:
www.nfpa.org/PDF/nfpa1600.pdf?src=nfpa

Additional information on Community Preparedness and Participation can be found online at:
http://www.citizencorps.gov/

Additional information on the *Ready Campaign* can be found online at: http://www.ready.gov/

5.0   A NATIONAL PREPAREDNESS SYSTEM SUPPORTS THE GUIDELINES

"We must now translate [these National Preparedness Guidelines] into a robust preparedness system that includes integrated plans, procedures, policies, training, and capabilities at all levels of government. The System must also incorporate the private sector, nongovernmental organizations, faith-based groups, and communities, including individual citizens."
        – The Federal Response to Hurricane Katrina, Lessons Learned, February 2006

The National Preparedness System provides a way to organize preparedness activities and programs pursuant to the *National Preparedness Guidelines* (see Figure 6). The desired end-state of our National Preparedness System is to achieve and sustain coordinated capabilities to prevent, protect against, respond to, and recover from all hazards in a way that balances risk with resources.

Figure 6: National Preparedness System

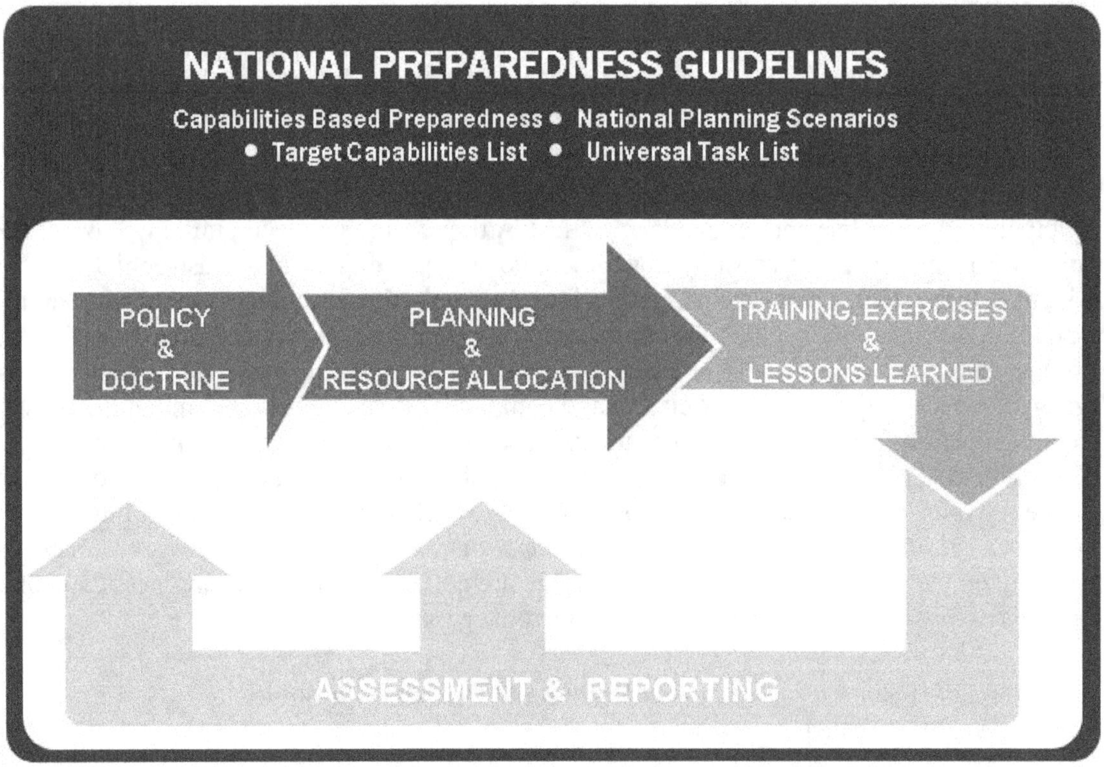

The National Preparedness System provides opportunities for all levels of government, the private sector, nongovernmental organizations, and individual citizens to work together to achieve priorities and capabilities outlined in the *Guidelines*. Many actions will be concurrent. They are described below in order of sequence:

- **Policy and Doctrine** involves ongoing management and maintenance of national policy and doctrine for operations and preparedness, such as the NIMS, NRP, NIPP, and the *Guidelines*.

- **Planning and Resource Allocation** involves application of common planning processes and tools by government officials, working with the private sector, nongovernmental organizations, and individual citizens to identify requirements, allocate resources, and build and maintain coordinated capabilities that are prioritized based upon risk.

- **Training, Exercises, and Lessons Learned** involves delivery of training and exercises and performance evaluation to identify lessons learned and share effective practices.

- **Assessment and Reporting** involves assessments based on established readiness metrics and reporting on progress and effectiveness of efforts to achieve the vision of the *Guidelines*.

6.0 MANAGEMENT AND MAINTENANCE

Because the *Guidelines* will be implemented over time through a wide range of preparedness programs and activities, they do not include specific implementation instructions (guidance on institutionalizing the *Guidelines* is within the Letter of Instruction at Appendix A). Guidance on *Guidelines* implementation will also be supported by changes in requirements for receiving Federal preparedness assistance, annual Federal program guidance, and Federal regulations, to the extent permitted by law. Many programs and activities are already consistent with the *Guidelines* and simply need to be implemented in closer coordination. Other partners might need to initiate or reorient programs and initiatives (along with measurable objectives) to implement the *Guidelines*. Implementation and partner feedback will inform future refinements to the *Guidelines*. DHS will coordinate the establishment of a national-level structure and process for the ongoing management and maintenance of the *Guidelines*. This will be closely coordinated with similar structures and processes for the NIMS, NRP, NIPP, and other elements of the National Preparedness System in order to help ensure national policy and planning for operations and preparedness are mutually supportive.

DHS is committed to working with its homeland security partners in updating and maintaining the *Guidelines* and related documents as part of a unified National Preparedness System, which will help ensure coordinated strategies, plans, procedures, policies, training, and capabilities at all levels of government. Implementation of the National Preparedness System is well under way. It is building on assessments of risk, development of management policies and strategies, identification of specific missions and supporting tasks in comprehensive plans, and matching of capabilities against requirements to execute these policies, strategies, and plans. Federal, State, local, tribal, and territorial governments will participate in assessments of readiness on a regular basis. The National Preparedness System will emphasize feedback and periodic reassessment to ensure the current state of preparedness is based on readiness metrics and is used as the basis for policy and programmatic decisions. HSPD-8 requires the Secretary of Homeland Security to provide to the President annual status reports on the Nation's level of preparedness, including State capabilities, the readiness of Federal civil response assets, the utilization of mutual aid, and an assessment of how Federal preparedness programs support the *Guidelines*. These reports will contribute to updates of the *Guidelines*.

APPENDIX A – LETTER OF INSTRUCTION

The National Preparedness Guidelines (*Guidelines*) are formally established upon issuance and supersede the Interim National Preparedness Goal issued on March 31, 2005. The *Guidelines* provide an overarching vision, tools, and priorities to shape national preparedness. The *Guidelines* do not include an implementation plan; implementation will occur over time through a wide range of Federal, State, local, tribal, and territorial preparedness programs and activities. For example, Federal program offices will develop detailed plans that describe how their programs support *Guidelines* implementation in consultation with their stakeholders. Those details must be reflected in annual program guidance, in the form of measurable objectives and requirements. DHS will monitor those efforts and advise program offices and DHS leadership on progress and opportunities to improve synchronization. Implementation and feedback will inform future refinement of the *Guidelines*.

Requirements

This section outlines roles and responsibilities of Federal, State, local, tribal, and territorial governments, nongovernmental organizations, the private sector, and citizens in implementing the preparedness framework outlined by the *Guidelines*. Specifically, this section provides examples of potential activities for the purpose of outlining the way forward. *Guidelines* implementation will also be supported by changes in requirements for receiving Federal preparedness assistance, annual Federal program guidance, and Federal regulations to the extent permitted by law. Many programs and activities are already consistent with the *Guidelines* and simply need to be implemented in closer coordination. Nothing in HSPD-8 alters or impedes the ability of government officials to perform their responsibilities under law.

Department of Homeland Security

As the lead for implementation of the preparedness framework outlined by the *Guidelines*, DHS shall do the following:

- Coordinate the establishment of a management and maintenance structure and process for the *Guidelines*, including the Capabilities-Based Preparedness tools and the assessment system;

- As outlined in HSPD-8, coordinate consistency with the *Guidelines* among Federal departments and agencies associated with the following:

    - Federal preparedness assistance;

    - First responder equipment standards;

    - Preparedness research and development activities;

    - Federal training programs;

    - National Exercise Program;

    - Interagency planning processes;

    - Performance measurements for national preparedness;

    - Relevant Federal regulatory requirements; and

    - Federal assets in support of State, local, territorial, and tribal government operations.

- Address other HSPD-8 requirements, as appropriate.

State, Local, Tribal, and Territorial Governments and Nongovernmental Organizations

State, local, tribal, and territorial governments and nongovernmental organizations are encouraged to do the following:

- Participate in the development and implementation of the management and maintenance structure and process for the *Guidelines*, including the Capabilities-Based Preparedness tools and the assessment system;
- Participate in *Guidelines* implementation by ascertaining their capability levels and their respective requirements, and by consulting in the development of program plans and guidance documents;
- Adopt a step-by-step capability preparedness process similar to that described in Appendix B to ensure that their respective homeland security programs are administered in a manner that is consistent with the *Guidelines* and enhance the National Priorities;
- Participate in regional initiatives to identify and synchronize the availability of existing and future capabilities that may be accessible through mutual aid agreements;
- Define appropriate support roles for employees to perform as emergency staff to fulfill capabilities, and support the development and maintenance of an inventory of capabilities; and
- Address other HSPD-8 requirements as appropriate.

Private Sector

As stated in HSPD-8, appropriate private sector entities are encouraged to do the following:

- Incorporate the safety and security of people and assets into business plans and corporate strategies;
- Participate in the development and implementation of the management and maintenance structure and process for the *Guidelines*, including the Capabilities-Based Preparedness tools and the assessment system;
- Participate in *Guidelines* implementation by determining requirements and achieving capabilities, and by consulting in the development of program plans and guidance documents;
- Participate in State, local, tribal, territorial, and regional planning and assessment processes to comply with the *Guidelines* and TCL; and
- Address other HSPD-8 requirements as appropriate.

As stated in HSPD-7, private sector entities are encouraged to do the following:

- Work with the relevant Sector-Specific Agencies to identify, prioritize, and coordinate the protection of critical infrastructure and key resources in conformance with the National Infrastructure Protection Plan; and

- Share information about physical and cyber threats, vulnerabilities, incidents, potential protective measures, and effective practices.

Federal Departments and Agencies

To support the Federal role in implementing the preparedness framework outlined in the *Guidelines*, Federal departments and agencies (including DHS) shall do the following:

- Support and participate in the management and maintenance structure and process developed for the *Guidelines*, associated tools, and Capabilities-Based Preparedness process;

- Initiate or re-orient programs and initiatives (along with measurable objectives) to implement the *Guidelines*. The following step-by-step process is suggested for use by Federal departments and agencies to ensure that their respective homeland security assistance programs are administered in a manner that is consistent with the *Guidelines* and enhances the National Priorities. This process description will be refined over time with user feedback and supplemented with specific instructions, if necessary and if requested. This process is *not* intended to substitute or impede department or agency autonomy for determining *how* individual programs and initiatives will be modified to help implement the *Guidelines*:

  o *Step 1: Analyze the Guidelines and Identify Applicable Programs* – Review the *Guidelines* to understand the intent, direction, and requirements for national preparedness. Identify preparedness programs – including initiatives to address Hurricane Katrina Lessons Learned – that are applicable to the *Guidelines*. A program or initiative is applicable to the *Guidelines* if its objectives support any of the National Priorities or the capabilities identified in the TCL. Applicable programs and initiatives may consist of grants, training, exercises, equipment, technical assistance, and response capabilities to Federal, State, local, tribal, territorial, nongovernmental, or private sector entities. Departments and agencies will periodically update and communicate to DHS (as requested) this inventory of programs and initiatives, along with their status in supporting the *Guidelines*. This information will be used for the Annual Report to the President on National Preparedness;

  o *Step 2: Assess Program and Guidelines Consistency* – Assess the services provided by each applicable program or initiative to determine their consistency with the *Guidelines*. Details on relevant programs and initiatives should be shared and coordinated with DHS and the Homeland Security Council (HSC) to ensure an integrated approach and action plan for *Guidelines* implementation. The HSC is responsible for coordinating the development of national homeland security policy. DHS, with oversight from the HSC, is responsible for coordinating the development and implementation of homeland security program plans and annual program guidance among Federal departments and agencies. Compliant Federal programs shall define interconnected and complementary objectives, timelines, and requirements designed to synchronize with the *Guidelines*;

o ***Step 3: Align Guidelines Implementation with Budget and Program Schedules*** – To the greatest extent possible, Federal departments and agencies should modify applicable program plans and policies to be consistent with the *Guidelines*. Federal departments and agencies should notify DHS of program reforms that cannot be completed in the upcoming budget cycle and should begin the process for implementing reforms in future-year budget cycles in a manner that comports with their overall mission priorities;

o ***Step 4: Modify Applicable Programs*** – Each applicable program should conform its operations to be consistent with the *Guidelines*. Conformance with the *Guidelines* may warrant reforms to the administration, goals, objectives, accompanying guidance, published materials, permitted uses, application process, award criteria, and other components of the applicable program. Conformance will also necessitate the integration of quantifiable preparedness and performance measures outlined in the TCL within relevant applicable programs – including applications, award criteria, and project evaluations – to monitor the progress of the program and its beneficiaries to advance the *Guidelines*. Federal departments and agencies should modify application and award processes to adopt the Capabilities-Based Preparedness process (See Appendix B) and to monitor and report the application of applicable homeland security programs in furtherance of the priorities and capabilities set forth in the *Guidelines* and TCL;

o ***Step 5: Notify Stakeholders*** – As soon as it is practicable, notify all appropriate partners and beneficiaries of the applicable preparedness and response programs about the reforms and their corresponding relationship to the *Guidelines*, TCL, and national initiatives. Such notice may also include a solicitation of comments and suggestions for future changes to the *Guidelines* and TCL;

o ***Step 6: Maintenance*** – Monitor the administration of the applicable programs to ensure that they support the *Guidelines*. Participate in the DHS management and maintenance process by submitting suggestions and comments to DHS. Comments may include any function of reforming applicable programs to the *Guidelines* and should specifically identify inconsistencies with other ongoing initiatives, implementation difficulties, and recommended modifications to the TCL to ensure that it represents the most current means of measuring national preparedness. Agencies should identify how relevant data on program priorities, performance measures, and capability assessments will be collected and integrated with national reporting efforts;

▪ Support the development and maintenance of an inventory of Federal programs that support capabilities outlined in the *Guidelines*; and

▪ Address other HSPD-8 requirements as appropriate.

Citizens

As directed in HSPD-8, DHS will work with all levels of government, nongovernmental organizations, and the private sector to encourage active citizen participation and involvement in preparedness. DHS along with Federal, State, local, tribal and territorial governments, and private and nonprofit sectors should focus on efforts to accomplish the following:

- Integrate and institutionalize citizen participation in all homeland security efforts nationwide;

- Support a culture of preparedness by fostering collaboration and integration of all community resources (citizens, nongovernmental organizations, private sector, and faith-based organizations) with preparedness efforts at all levels of government through mechanisms, such as Citizen Corps Councils, to conduct awareness and outreach campaigns to deliver the message of personal responsibility to "prepare, train, and volunteer," and to motivate all Americans to take action to reduce their vulnerability and increase resilience;

- Encourage citizen training and volunteer opportunities through programs such as Community Emergency Response Teams, Medical Reserve Corps, Fire Corps, Volunteers in Police Service, Neighborhood Watch, Citizens' Academy, Ready Kids, and Ready Business;

- Focus on special needs populations, such as people with disabilities, language and cultural differences, economic barriers, and age-related issues and concerns;

- Develop standards, recognition incentives, and assessment and evaluation criteria for citizen preparedness and participation;

- Share lessons learned and effective practices from communities around the country; and

- Identify Cabinet Secretaries and other prominent public figures to serve as spokespersons to promote citizen and community preparedness.

APPENDIX B – CAPABILITIES-BASED PREPAREDNESS OVERVIEW

The *National Preparedness Guidelines* (*Guidelines*) are supported by a capabilities-based approach to planning for major events. Capabilities-Based Preparedness is a form of all-hazards planning. This Appendix provides an overview of Capabilities-Based Preparedness and outlines a process that Federal, State, regional, and local preparedness programs can utilize as Capabilities-Based Preparedness is adopted and institutionalized nationwide. It is organized into three sections:

1. Definition
2. Planning Tools Referenced in the *Guidelines*
3. Capabilities-Based Preparedness Process

1. Definition

Capabilities-Based Preparedness is defined as:

> *...preparing, under uncertainty, to provide capabilities suitable for a wide range of challenges while working within an economic framework that necessitates prioritization and choice.*

Capabilities-Based Preparedness is a way to make informed choices about how to manage the risk and reduce the impact posed by potential threats. It focuses decision making on building and maintaining <u>capabilities</u> to prevent and protect against challenges (e.g., intelligence analysis, critical infrastructure protection, etc.) and to respond and recover when events occur (e.g., onsite incident management, medical surge, emergency public information, and economic recovery). The process rests on a foundation of multi-disciplinary, cross-governmental, and regional collaboration to determine measurable capability targets, to assess current levels of capabilities, and to find ways to close the gaps. As entities make choices in preparedness programs and activities, they will be able to improve their own preparedness, focus available assistance on areas of greatest need, and collaborate with others using a common reference framework.

Capabilities are defined as providing:

> *...the means to accomplish a mission or function and achieve desired outcomes by performing critical tasks, under specified conditions, to target levels of performance.*

The 37 capabilities referenced in the *Guidelines* span the full spectrum of homeland security missions. While the listing does not yet encompass every function that must be accomplished to prevent, protect against, respond to, or recover from a major event, it nonetheless offers a comprehensive starting point for planning. Each capability is described in detail in the Target Capabilities List (TCL), which accompanies the *Guidelines*. The description includes a definition, outcome, preparedness and performance activities, tasks, and measures.

2.   Planning Tools Referenced in the *Guidelines*

The *National Preparedness Guidelines* utilize and reference three Capabilities-Based Preparedness tools: the National Planning Scenarios, the TCL, and the Universal Task List (UTL).

National Planning Scenarios

While preparedness applies across the all-hazards spectrum, the 2002 National Strategy for Homeland Security attaches special emphasis to preparing for catastrophic threats with "the greatest risk of mass casualties, massive property loss, and immense social disruption." To illustrate the potential scope, magnitude, and complexity of a range of major events, the Homeland Security Council—in partnership with the Department of Homeland Security (DHS), other Federal departments and agencies, and State, local, tribal, and territorial governments— developed the National Planning Scenarios. The 15 Scenarios include terrorist attacks, major disasters, and other emergencies. They are listed in Figure B-1.

Figure B-1: National Planning Scenarios

National Planning Scenarios	
Improvised Nuclear Device	Major Earthquake
Aerosol Anthrax	Major Hurricane
Pandemic Influenza	Radiological Dispersal Device
Plague	Improvised Explosive Device
Blister Agent	Food Contamination
Toxic Industrial Chemicals	Foreign Animal Disease
Nerve Agent	Cyber Attack
Chlorine Tank Explosion	

All levels of government can use the National Planning Scenarios as a reference to explore the potential consequences of major events and to evaluate and improve their capabilities to perform their assigned missions and tasks. Planners are not precluded from developing their own scenarios to supplement the National Planning Scenarios. DHS will maintain a National Planning Scenario portfolio and update it periodically based on changes in the homeland security strategic environment. The current version is available on the Office of Domestic Preparedness (ODP) Secure Portal (https://odp.esportals.com) and the Lessons Learned Information Sharing system (https://www.llis.dhs.gov). Use of specific National Planning Scenarios in federally funded training and exercises will be addressed in program guidance.

Target Capabilities List

The TCL identifies and defines capabilities that the Nation may need to achieve and sustain, depending on relevant risks and threats, in order to be prepared. A capability may be delivered with any combination of properly planned, organized, equipped, trained, and exercised personnel that achieves the desired outcome. Entities are expected to develop and maintain capabilities at levels that reflect the differing risk and needs across the country.

Each capability includes a description of the major activities performed within the capability and the critical tasks and measures associated with the activity. Critical tasks are those tasks that must be performed during a major event in order to minimize the impact on lives, property, and the economy. Critical tasks may require coordination among Federal, State, local, tribal, territorial, private sector, and/or nongovernmental entities during their execution. They are essential to achieving the desired outcome and to the success of a homeland security mission. The critical tasks are derived from the tasks found in the UTL. Critical tasks, when linked to operating conditions and performance standards, provide the primary source of learning objectives for training and exercises and provide input to planning and performance evaluation. Operating conditions are variables of the environment, such as the terrain, weather, presence of an adversary, and complexity of multi-agency relationships, that may affect performance. The TCL includes measures and metrics that are quantitative or qualitative levels against which achievement of a task or capability outcome can be assessed.

Planners at all levels of government can use the TCL as a reference to help them design plans, procedures, training, and exercises that develop capacity and proficiency to perform their assigned missions and tasks in major events. The TCL was developed with Federal, State, and local subject-matter experts and drew on existing sources wherever possible. It will be updated periodically in conjunction with the UTL. The current version is available on the ODP secure portal (https://odp.esportals.com) and the Lessons Learned Information Sharing system (https://www.llis.dhs.gov).

Universal Task List

The UTL provides a menu of tasks required to prevent, protect against, respond to, and recover from major events represented by the National Planning Scenarios. Most tasks are common to many, if not all, of the Scenarios, as well as other events not covered by the Scenarios. The UTL serves as a common language and reference system that will support efforts to describe operational tasks, so that personnel from across the Nation can work together effectively when required. No single entity is expected to perform every task.

The UTL was developed with Federal, State, local, tribal, territorial, private sector, and nongovernmental subject-matter experts and drew on existing sources wherever possible. The UTL will be updated periodically in conjunction with the TCL. The current version is available on the ODP secure portal (https://odp.esportals.com) and the Lessons Learned Information Sharing system (https://www.llis.dhs.gov).

3.   Capabilities-Based Preparedness Process

The Capabilities-Based Preparedness process (see Figure B-2) involves homeland security partners in a systematic and prioritized effort to accomplish the following:

- Convene working groups;
- Determine capability requirements;
- Assess current capability levels;
- Identify, analyze, and choose options;

- Update plans and strategies;
- Allocate funds;
- Update and execute program plans; and
- Assess and report.

The process emphasizes collaboration to identify, achieve, and sustain target levels of capability that will contribute to enhancing overall national levels of preparedness. This simple, step-by-step sequence illustrates how processes and tools are combined to identify and prioritize measurable preparedness targets in assessing current capabilities, then allocating available resources and emphasis to the most urgently needed capabilities based on risk. DHS will refine this description over time with user feedback and supplement it with specific instructions in annual program guidance.

Figure B-2: Capabilities-Based Preparedness Process

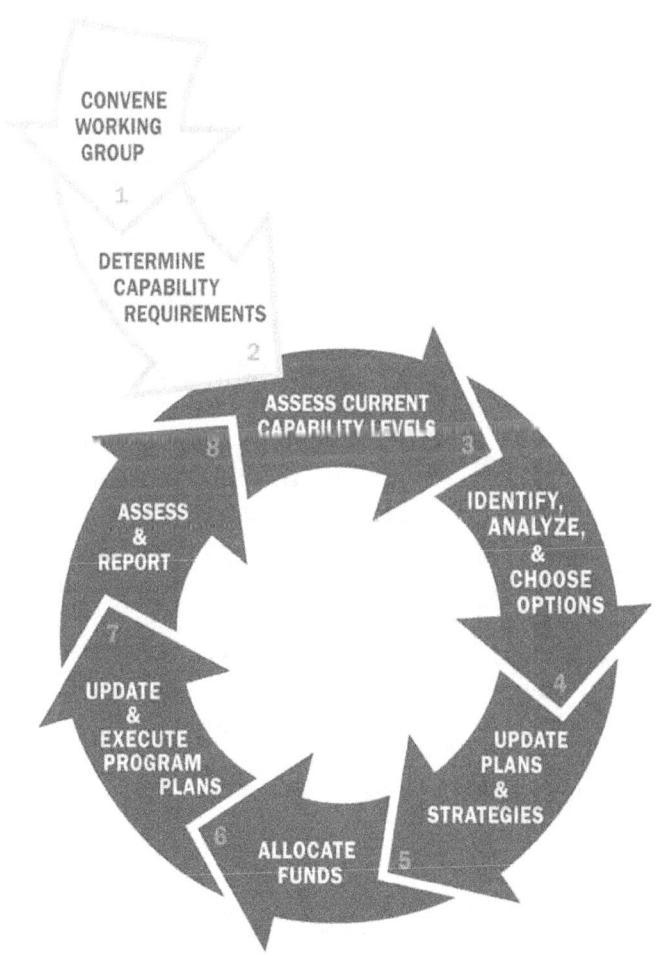

Step 1: Convene Working Group

The preparedness process should begin with formation of a chartered, representative working group. It is strongly encouraged that, wherever possible, previously established working groups be used for this process. The working group should be multi-disciplinary, multi-agency, and multi-jurisdictional. Where appropriate, working groups should include the private sector and nongovernmental partners. The intent is to bring together regional practitioners from across disciplines so that they can be effective advisors to the senior decision-makers who formulate strategies, set priorities, and allocate funds.

Step 2: Determine Capability Targets

The working group will determine risk-based target levels for each capability by reviewing the TCL and conducting risk analysis. Such target levels must balance risk with resources – both resources that are currently available and those that can realistically be acquired through regional collaboration.

The TCL provides a series of examples of how capabilities may apply to jurisdictions of different sizes. These examples are intended to provide guidance on how the target levels listed in individual capabilities vary based on the region and implementing agency. It is important to keep in mind that *any* combination of elements (or resources) that delivers the desired outcome is acceptable. The TCL is *not* intended to direct specific resource requirements for every agency or jurisdiction for each year, nor is it descriptive of all of the resources necessary for every type of scenario.

Step 3: Assess Current Capability Levels

The core of the Capabilities-Based Preparedness approach is the comparison of current capabilities with risk-based target capability levels. The working group will coordinate an assessment of the current levels of capability. Capability assessments measure the current level of capability against the target levels of capability from the TCL applicable to the respective level of government. Comparisons will reveal "gaps" (implying outcomes cannot be accomplished with current capabilities), "excesses" (unnecessary redundancies or no longer needed capabilities), and "deficiencies" (an existing capability that is insufficient to provide a reasonable assurance of success against a specified scenario). Some of the required capabilities and expertise will not be present in the State or jurisdiction. Many will be secured through regional multi-agency coordination (i.e., mutual aid, acquisition through contracting, and resources from nongovernmental and private sector partners).

Step 4: Identify, Analyze, and Choose Options

Capabilities-Based Preparedness also involves selecting methods to address capability gaps and deficiencies. This step involves translating a capability gap or deficiency into specific needs and determining a combination of resources to fulfill the need. Analytical processes using comparative, trade-off, and risk analyses are applied in this step. Recognizing that there is usually more than one resource combination that can address a capability gap or deficiency, the analysis includes identifying, analyzing, and choosing options, using the recommended resources identified in the TCL as a guide. This analysis provides senior decision-makers with alternative combinations of resources or solution sets for each capability gap or deficiency. Analysis components are described below.

Identify Options. The range of options identified should be kept to a manageable number, but solutions should be framed in terms of the elements required to implement a capability. A capability may be delivered with any combination of properly planned, organized, equipped, trained, and exercised personnel that achieves the desired outcome. In reviewing options, the effectiveness of applying mutual aid among geographic regions and levels of government should be considered.

Analyze Options. Once a range of options has been identified, each option should be analyzed and prioritized against a standard set of criteria. The analysis will determine the combination of resources that could provide the desired capability or capabilities and will appropriately address risk. Examples of criteria include the following:

- Ability of the identified approaches to provide the desired capability. Due to prior investments, it may not be necessary to invest in all six elements (see Figure 3 on page 5 of the *Guidelines*) at one time in order to achieve a capability;

- Ability of the approaches to deliver the total capability. If an approach cannot deliver the total capability, evaluate how much of the capability can be met;

- Delivery time frame;

- Relative improvement in capability level provided by the approaches as compared to the existing capability; and

- Cost to develop, procure, and sustain the approaches versus the cost to sustain the existing capability.

Choose Options. The results of the analysis are presented to senior decision-makers for consideration. Risk determinations are embedded in the decision-making process. Risk determinations will consider the range of capability gaps, excesses, and deficiencies; issues identified during analysis (as identified in the analyze options component criteria); and strategic concerns and implications. Risk determinations will also consider the following:

- Can the capability outcome be accomplished and provide a reasonable assurance of success?

- What are the potential costs compared to other options? Are the costs and time required appropriate for the benefit gained?

- What is the impact on planning? Is the solution compatible with other solutions available through assistance programs, and can mutual aid be applied to meet the requirement?

By applying known constraints and examining all capabilities, a preferred solution set can be selected. The results can then be consolidated into a prioritized, balanced portfolio across all relevant capabilities.

Step 5: Update Plans and Strategies

Once options are chosen, working groups can update their emergency operations plans and preparedness strategies. The strategies should be aligned with the *National Preparedness Guidelines* and support and facilitate regional cooperation and mutual aid. Strategies are multi-year planning vehicles supported by specific annual work plans that describe each year's approach to meeting the longer term strategy. Regional mutual aid agreements should be updated or revised, funding requests should identify prioritized resource needs, and existing resources should be reallocated, as appropriate, to close capability gaps.

Step 6: Allocate Resources

Decision-makers will lead a review of budgets, existing resources, and funding requests and map these to current or potential sources of funding. Using Capabilities-Based Preparedness, their aim is to produce an effective and regionally coordinated preparedness portfolio within each jurisdiction and, as a consequence, across the Nation. Ultimately, balancing the preparedness portfolio will contribute to a more prepared Nation by accomplishing the following:

- Maximizing the return on preparedness investments and resources in compliance with homeland security strategies and in coordination with the *National Preparedness Guidelines*;

- Providing clarity in resource allocation decisions based on consistently applied criteria and decision-making frameworks; and

- Encouraging a regional and/or mutual aid partner approach to national preparedness.

Step 7: Update and Execute Program Plans

The strategies and plans previously developed and/or updated are implemented through the execution step. All relevant stakeholders carry out annual work plans. Execution focuses on the following:

- Administering programs;
- Conducting planning and coordination;
- Purchasing equipment in accordance with documented needs and specified standards, as well as preparing and maintaining such equipment to be readily available as needed;
- Developing and conducting training to fill capability gaps; and
- Developing and conducting exercises to demonstrate performance.

The following example describes how Step 7 applies to Training and Exercises.

Capabilities-Based Preparedness for Training and Exercises

- Review relevant strategy and policy to identify priority TCL capabilities to be trained for and exercised against

- Develop a Multi-Year Training and Exercise Plan and Schedule for intended training and exercise activities

- Per the Multi-Year Schedule, carry out planned training activities oriented toward augmenting priority TCL capabilities

- Conduct exercises that apply and evaluate the priority TCL capabilities developed through training

- Use a "building-block cycle" of escalating exercise complexity (e.g., tabletop exercise, followed by a drill, followed by a full-scale exercise) to incrementally build priority TCL capability levels

- Evaluate capabilities tested in exercises using Homeland Security Exercise and Evaluation Program Exercise Evaluation Guides linked to each TCL capability

- Update Multi-Year Plan annually to reflect new priority capabilities and lessons learned from exercises

For more on Capabilities-Based Preparedness Planning for training and exercises, see *Homeland Security Exercise and Evaluation Program Volume I: Overview and Exercise Program Management* (http://hseep.dhs.gov).

Step 8: Assess and Report

An assessment process provides a continuously validated baseline for preparedness. Capability, compliance, and performance assessments provide the basis to determine preparedness of individual partners and levels of government, the synthesis of which produces a national assessment of preparedness. Capability assessments are discussed in Step 3. Other types of assessments include performance and compliance assessments. Performance and compliance assessments serve to validate levels of capability. Compliance assessments will provide insight into conformance with requirements (e.g., NIMS and other national programs). Performance assessments are conducted through exercise programs.

Assessments are performed on a regular basis. Information from these assessments provides comprehensive indicators for how effectively capabilities are achieved and maintained within the assessed region. The results of these assessments will be presented to relevant decision-makers for use as a mechanism to develop subsequent guidance. Analysis from assessments will enable relevant decision-makers to ensure the appropriate balance of resources allocated to strengthen specific capabilities.

The synthesis of analyses will help to develop a comprehensive "snapshot" of preparedness. In addition to State and local efforts, overall progress towards increasing the national level of preparedness will be documented and communicated through a national reporting cycle and Annual Status Report.

The desired end-state is to implement the vision of preparedness defined in the *National Preparedness Guidelines* and to coordinate homeland security capabilities across jurisdictions and disciplines. Information from Capabilities-Based Preparedness will be used by preparedness programs at all levels of government to refine program structures and strategies. This requires understanding capability needs at the national level through analysis of data collected nationwide. Results will be used to update the national priorities in the *Guidelines* and to provide enhanced strategic direction for the Nation.

Achieving national preparedness hinges on using a flexible, all-hazards process that provides common objectives, priorities, and standards. Capabilities-Based Preparedness provides the means to address a wide range of challenges by leveraging appropriate homeland security programs to reach our destination – A Nation Prepared.

APPENDIX C – TERMS AND DEFINITIONS

All-Hazards Preparedness. Refers to preparedness for terrorist attacks, major disasters, and other emergencies within the United States. (Source: HSPD-8, December 17, 2003)

Capability. A capability provides the means to accomplish a mission or function resulting from the performance of one or more critical tasks, under specified conditions, to target levels of performance. A capability may be delivered with *any* combination of properly planned, organized, equipped, trained, and exercised personnel that achieves the desired outcome.

Critical Infrastructure. Critical infrastructure is defined as systems and assets, whether physical or virtual, so vital to the United States that the incapacity or destruction of such systems and assets would have a debilitating impact on any combination of national security, national economic security, or national public health or safety. (Source: USA PATRIOT Act of 2001 and Homeland Security Act of 2002, 6 U.S.C. § 101 *et seq.*)

Critical Tasks. Critical tasks are those tasks essential to achieving success in a homeland security mission for a major event to prevent an occurrence, to minimize loss of life and serious injuries, or to mitigate significant property damage.

Emergency. As defined by the *Robert T. Stafford Disaster Relief and Emergency Assistance Act* (42 U.S.C. § 5121 *et seq.*), an emergency means any occasion or instance for which, in the determination of the President, Federal assistance is needed to supplement State and local efforts and capabilities to save lives and to protect property and public health and safety or to lessen or avert the threat of a catastrophe in any part of the United States. (Source: NRP, December 2004)

Federal Departments and Agencies. Those executive departments enumerated in 5 U.S.C. 101; independent establishments as defined by 5 U.S.C. § 104(1); government corporations as defined by 5 U.S.C. § 103(1); and the United States Postal Service. (Source: HSPD-8, December 17, 2003)

First Responder. Local and nongovernmental police, fire, and other emergency personnel who, in the early stages of an incident, are responsible for the protection and preservation of life, property, evidence, and the environment. This includes emergency response providers as defined in section 2 of the Homeland Security Act of 2002, as well as emergency management, public health, clinical care, public works, and other skilled support personnel (such as equipment operators) who provide immediate support services during prevention, response, and recovery operations. First responders may include personnel from Federal, State, local, tribal, territorial, or nongovernmental organizations. (Source: NRP, December 2004)

Jurisdiction. A range or sphere of authority. Public agencies have jurisdiction at an incident related to their legal responsibilities and authority. Jurisdictional authority at an incident can be political or geographic (e.g., city, county, territorial, tribal, State, or Federal boundary lines) or functional (e.g., law enforcement, public health). (Source: NIMS, March 2004)

Key Resources. Key resources are defined as "publicly or privately controlled resources essential to the minimal operations of the economy and government." (Source: Homeland Security Act of 2002)

Local Government. Local is defined as "(A) a county, municipality, city, town, township, local public authority, school district, special district, intrastate district, council of governments (regardless of whether the council of governments is incorporated as a nonprofit corporation under State law), regional or interstate government entity, or agency or instrumentality of a local government; (B) an Indian tribe or authorized tribal organization, or in Alaska a Native village or Alaska Regional Native Corporation; and (C) a rural community, unincorporated town or village, or other public entity." (Source: Homeland Security Act of 2002)

Major Disaster. As defined under the *Robert T. Stafford Disaster Relief and Emergency Assistance Act (42 U.S.C. 5122)*, a major disaster is any natural catastrophe (including any hurricane, tornado, storm, high water, wind-driven water, tidal wave, tsunami, earthquake, volcanic eruption, landslide, mudslide, snowstorm, or drought) or, regardless of cause, any fire, flood, or explosion, in any part of the United States, which in the determination of the President causes damage of sufficient severity and magnitude to warrant major disaster assistance under this act to supplement the efforts and available resources of States, local governments, and disaster relief organizations to alleviate the damage, loss, hardship, or suffering caused thereby. (Source: NIMS, March 2004)

Major Event. Refers to terrorist attacks, major disasters, and other emergencies within the United States. (Source: HSPD-8, December 17, 2003)

Mass Prophylaxis. The process by which an entire community is to receive prophylactic drugs and vaccines over a defined period of time in response to possible exposure to a biological agent. (Source: Community-Based Mass Prophylaxis – A Planning Guide for Public Health Preparedness, Agency for Healthcare Research and Quality, August 2004)

Measures and Metrics. Performance measures of quantitative or qualitative levels against which achievement of a task or capability outcome can be assessed. They describe how much, how well, and/or how quickly an action should be performed and are typically expressed in way that can be observed during an exercise or real event. The measures and metrics are not standards. They serve as guides for planning, training, and exercise activities. However, nationally accepted standards of performance, benchmarks, and guidelines are reflected, if applicable. (Source: Target Capabilities List, March 2007)

Mitigation. The activities designed to reduce or eliminate risks to persons or property or to lessen the actual or potential effects or consequences of an incident. Mitigation measures may be implemented prior to, during, or after an incident. Mitigation measures are often informed by lessons learned from prior incidents. Mitigation involves ongoing actions that reduce exposure to, probability of, or potential loss from hazards. Measures may include zoning and building codes, floodplain buyouts, and analysis of hazard-related data to determine where it is safe to build or locate temporary facilities. Mitigation can include efforts to educate governments, businesses, and the public on measures they can take to reduce loss and injury. (Source: NIMS, March 2004)

National. Of a nationwide character, including the Federal, State, local, tribal, and territorial aspects of governance and policy. (Source: NIMS, March 2004)

Preparedness. The range of deliberate, critical tasks and activities necessary to build, sustain, and improve the operational capability to prevent, protect against, respond to, and recover from domestic incidents. Preparedness is a continuous process. Preparedness involves efforts at all levels of government and coordination among government, private-sector, and nongovernmental organizations to identify threats, determine vulnerabilities, and identify required resources. Within the NIMS, preparedness is operationally focused on establishing guidelines, protocols, and standards for planning, training and exercises, personnel qualification and certification, equipment certification, and publication management. (Source: NIMS, March 2004)

Prevention. Actions to avoid an incident or to intervene to stop an incident from occurring. Prevention involves actions taken to protect lives and property. It involves applying intelligence and other information to a range of activities that may include such countermeasures as deterrence operations; heightened inspections; improved surveillance and security operations; investigations to determine the full nature and source of the threat; public health and agricultural surveillance and testing processes; immunizations, isolation, or quarantine; and, as appropriate, specific law enforcement operations aimed at deterring, preempting, interdicting, or disrupting illegal activity and apprehending potential perpetrators and bringing them to justice. Under HSPD-8, the *National Preparedness Guidelines* do not address more general and broader prevention efforts to deter, disrupt, or thwart terrorism by Federal law enforcement, defense, and intelligence agencies. (Source: NIMS, March 2004; HSPD-8, December 17, 2003)

Protection. Actions to reduce the vulnerability of critical infrastructure or key resources in order to deter, mitigate, or neutralize terrorist attacks, major disasters, and other emergencies. It requires coordinated action on the part of Federal, State, and local governments, the private sector, and concerned citizens across the country. Protection also includes continuity of government and operations planning; awareness elevation and understanding of threats and vulnerabilities to their critical facilities, systems, and functions; identification and promotion of effective sector-specific protection practices and methodologies; and expansion of voluntary security-related information sharing among private entities within the sector as well as between government and private entities. (Source: HSPD-7, December 17, 2003).

Recovery. The development, coordination, and execution of service and site restoration plans; the reconstitution of government operations and services; individual, private-sector, nongovernmental, and public assistance programs to provide housing and promote restoration; long-term care and treatment of affected persons; additional measures for social, political, environmental, and economic restoration; evaluation of the incident to identify lessons learned; post-incident reporting; and development of initiatives to mitigate the effects of future incidents. (Source: NIMS, March 2004)

Region. Generally refers to a geographic area consisting of contiguous Federal, State, local, territorial, and tribal entities.

Response. Activities that address the short-term, direct effects of an incident. Response includes immediate actions to save lives, protect property, and meet basic human needs. Response also includes the execution of emergency operations plans and of mitigation activities designed to limit the loss of life, personal injury, property damage, and other unfavorable outcomes. As indicated by the situation, response activities include applying intelligence and other information to lessen the effects or consequences of an incident; increased security operations; continuing investigations into the nature and source of the threat; ongoing public health and agricultural surveillance and testing processes; immunizations, isolation, or quarantine; and specific law enforcement operations aimed at preempting, interdicting, or disrupting illegal activity, apprehending actual perpetrators, and bringing them to justice. (Source: NIMS, March 2004)

Risk. Risk is a function of three variables: threat, vulnerability, and consequence. (Source: "Discussion of the FY 2006 Risk Methodology and the Urban Areas Security Initiative," November 2005, www.ojp.usdoj.gov/odp/docs/FY_2006_UASI_Program_ Explanation_Paper_011805.doc)

State Government. The governing body of any State of the United States, the District of Columbia, the Commonwealth of Puerto Rico, the Virgin Islands, Guam, American Samoa, the Commonwealth of the Northern Mariana Islands, and any possession of the United States. (Source: Homeland Security Act of 2002)

Volunteer. Any individual accepted to perform services by an agency that has the authority to accept volunteer services, if that individual performs services without promise, expectation, or receipt of compensation for services performed. (Source: NIMS, March 2004)

APPENDIX D – ACRONYMS AND ABBREVIATIONS

CBRNE	Chemical, Biological, Radiological, Nuclear, and Explosive
CDC	Centers for Disease Control and Prevention
CI/KR	Critical Infrastructure/Key Resources
CRI	Cities Readiness Initiative
DHS	Department of Homeland Security
DOJ	Department of Justice
EEG	Exercise Evaluation Guide
EMAC	Emergency Management Assistance Compact
EMS	Emergency Medical Services
FBI	Federal Bureau of Investigation
HHS	Department of Health and Human Services
HSPD	Homeland Security Presidential Directive
ICS	Incident Command System
IWN	Integrated Wireless Network
ISE	Information Sharing Environment
JTTF	Joint Terrorism Task Force
NEMA	National Emergency Management Association
NIMS	National Incident Management System
NIPP	National Infrastructure Protection Plan
NRP	National Response Plan
ODP	Office for Domestic Preparedness
SSP	Sector-Specific Plan
TCL	Target Capabilities List
UASI	Urban Areas Security Initiative
UTL	Universal Task List
WMD	Weapons of Mass Destruction